What Others Are Saying About This Book

"Thank you! Bless you for what you did over there. I'm sorry you had to go, but there are men alive today because you were there."
John Kerry, US Senator
Decorated Vietnam Veteran

"Penny's book brought back a lot of memories—of how many suffered in another war that never should have happened. Some of her poems are really gut-wrenching."
Pete McCloskey, Former US Congressman
Decorated Navy and Marine Corps Veteran

"It's time the hospital view comes to light."
John Murtha, US Congressman
Decorated Vietnam Veteran

"It provoked my fear and pain (from the VN War), which I had buried, in a beautiful and enlightened way. Thank you! I am so grateful and happy. Love does heal."
Iris Nu Dinh

"Too many of my guys needed who you were and what you did. Too many of my guys were your "Davey"."
P. Butler – Iraq and Afghanistan War Veteran

"Lt. Angel brought back a lot of old memories. My "Davey" was a Marine. I put my entire body and soul into his care but we couldn't save him You don't forget it EVER and you said it perfectly in your book. I am so sorry that a new generation has to go through it all again."

Don R. Goffinet, M.D., Vietnam Veteran

"Thank you for this important gift to humanity. I could not put the book down. I was intensely engaged in the imagery of the poems, narrative and "aftertaste" of each chapter. I felt elated, saddened, shocked, tearful, angry, sympathetic, reflective, and even somehow envious over the dynamic relationship you had with Davey and the powerful experiences that came from it. I think about our men and women currently in war and pray that each of them has a Lt Angel by their side."

Mark Stanford, PhD

"It is stunning, deeply moving, and extraordinary in the way that the most ordinary of people, like Davey, can be extraordinary in a way that profoundly changes others. You convey it all beautifully in the way you put this together. It is a treasure."

James Larocca, Two Time New York Gubernatorial Cabinet Member, Vietnam Veteran

"Nobody knows what you people went through. Our med units are smaller and better than I think you had, but what they see is the same. That's what doesn't change. I couldn't do what you did. I lost a leg. I can't imagine what you lost, but I know what you gave."

Brian – Iraq War Veteran

"What a magnificent book! It felt like Ms. Rock was talking directly to me and my only brother, who did four tours as a Marine in Vietnam. I was able to see my brother through her heart and eyes. I feel like Penny knew our family. Bless you, Ms. Rock! I salute you and say "Welcome Home" and many thanks from one USA citizen and sister. God bless Davey."

Kay Livingston

"With tears streaming down my face, I find it wonderful and amazing that I didn't hear the voice of hate in your writing, not for the Vietnamese or even our country. Truly your spirit seemed to be guided by love, for your patients, for Davey and yourself. And, it also helped me understand my father and his pain. This book is vital at this time in our history as we seem to be facing another situation where it seems there will be no winner, and only loss. I think at the end of things, that's really what makes a great life, knowing you made a difference for others."

Lisa Luttinger

"I could have used you over there. Friend or enemy, we all needed a Lt. Angel."

Jimmy – Iraq War Veteran

"I have never been able to cry over the loss I suffered until today. What a sweet relief, thank you. I can now grieve for my best friend that did not return and for my lover that did return. The latter went to Viet Nam full of love and kindness with his soul intact and came home with none of these gifts. Thank you for the reminder of what a glorious gift life is and that love does not die."

Kathleen Thomas

"Penny pulls no punches. Her words and images graphically depict the entire human experience and consequences of war."
Maureen Lynch

"I was deeply touched by your exquisite, amazing book and the candor in sharing such an intimate, private, and beautiful experience. Your messages need to be heard and felt. Such an insightful look into the potential in all of us to live in the power of love amidst the madness of war. I do not have the words to express how grateful I am that you are sharing this amazing experience with the rest of the world. You open the doors to mankind's innate capacity to live in the world of deep feelings and share those selflessly even with "strangers." You have done that with grace and beauty in a way that seems effortless."
Robert C. Kausen, President
Life Education, Inc.

"Thank you for your strength and your heart, for the songs to the soldiers, for your love, for telling the truth, for your courage and care for boys like my brother."
Mary Corral

"I wish I'd been able to read this before I went over there. It's the truth. Thank you."
J. Arnold – Iraq War Veteran

"Tears welled up in my eyes when I was reading your book and I realized just how young we all were. When I finished the book, I heard Placido Domingo on the radio singing "Always in My Heart". As it's the "essence" of your book, it also caused me to think about you singing—and how you must miss that."
      Phil Dynan, Author Brother Eagle–Sister Moon

"I can't tell you how much your book meant to me. I cried through the entire reading, I could not put it down until I finished it. I am a Combat Vet class of '65-'66. I know your pain, and felt it course through my body as I hung on to your every word. I haven't cried or felt the release of this pain until your book. Thank you."
              John Watson

"I want to thank you from the bottom of my heart. As a clinical psychologist and a former USAF officer who works with combat veterans and military sexual trauma veterans your words truly have a positive impact. I have heard my women veterans say, 'Penny is inspirational! Her words, her experience and perspective helps you feel there is hope that healing can happen. And that no matter what you have experienced in your life you can use those scars to better your life versus hide behind them—be proud of your scars and wounds to inspire you towards accomplishments versus being embarrassed by your scars and feeling less than."
Pamela Planthara, Clinical Psychologist Oakland Vet Center

"It's like an emotional travelogue from death to rebirth."
              James Shepard

"Thank you so very much for your sadly beautiful poems. As an Australian Vietnam Veteran, your words hit home like a barrage of mortar shells. Wounds and insidious effects of PTSD have plagued me since that time. There is power and healing contained in poetry. You find you are not alone in pain and suffering. That somebody else has experienced similarly and understands, is an emotional revelation."

Anthony W. Pahl, OAM

"Profoundly sad. Profoundly uplifting."

Tonya A.

"I'm sorry I didn't ask. I thought I was being kind. But, you were always in my mind and heart. Now I cry for soldiers who went—ones who came back and others still there. I cry for you. How did you create sanity for yourself? I love your book—packed with emotion. Such an uplifting, inspirational message."

Micki Hierl, Penny's Nursing School Roommate

He Called Me Lieutenant Angel

He Called Me Lieutenant Angel
A Love Song From War

Penny Rock

Penny Rock • Woodside, California

He Called Me Lieutenant Angel
A Love Song From War

By Penny Rock

Other works by Penny Rock:

CDs
Power of a Clear Mind: Keep Your Bearings in Any Circumstance
The 8 Essential Ingredients of Healing: From Anything, Anywhere, Anytime

Books
We Declare: The Truth About War and our Responsibility for Peace
Power of a Clear Mind: The Direct Link Between Your Leadership State of Mind, The Decisions You Make, The Actions You Take, The Results You Get
Available at www.powerofaclearmind.com

Published by: Penny Rock
www.powerofaclearmind.com

All rights reserved. No part of this book may be reproduced or transmitted in any form or by any means, electronic or mechanical, including photocopying, recording, or by any information storage and retrieval system, without written permission from the author, except for the inclusion of brief quotations in a review.

Copyright © 2006, 2008, 2010 by Penny Rock

ISBN 978-0-9787156-3-2

First Printing 2006
Second Printing 2008, revised
Third Printing 2010
Fourth Printing 2011

Printed in the United States of America

Cover Design by JD Buckwell
Author Photo by Terry Gardner
Vietnam Women's Memorial cover courtesy of Penny Rock
Back cover photo courtesy of Penny Rock

For Davey

> *"A hospital alone shows what war is."*
> ~ Erich Maria Remarque

Mr. Remarque understood that the confines of a hospital house the real story of war. The sights *after* the battle. The sights almost nobody sees in a lifetime. Inner city emergency rooms cannot compare. Movies don't even come close. The blood and guts are real, and glamour is nowhere to be found. No bugles blare to herald a pageant of glorious victory. Yet, in the midst of Dante's Inferno, Shangri La begins to appear. The story of Lieutenant Angel and Davey unfolded in such a place.

CONTENTS

Preface	**17**
Background	**19**
Remembering Davey	23
Penny's Dream	30
Davey's Dream	35
Introduction—It Begins at the End	**41**
I Sang You to Death	45
I Sang You to Death	47
Lieutenant Angel	49
Lieutenant Angel	50
The Days of War and Roses	**55**
Your Heart in My Grave	59
Your Favorite Rose	60
Let My Grave Stay Open	61
The Rose on Your Grave	62
My Sense of You	64
Last Moment	65
Eternal Connection	**67**
I Know You're With Me	70
One Breath Away	72
We Two are One	73
We'll Find Us	74
Hairpins on the Floor	75
She Waits for Him	77
Return to Me	79

What More Could I Do?	**81**
Lament	85
Davey's Waltz	88
Davey's Waltz	89
Life Interrupted	**93**
The War Got in the Way	96
The War Got in the Way	97
Funeral Plans	100
Funeral Plans	101
Penny's and Davey's Funeral Plans	104
A Lesson and A Promise	**107**
I Learned About Living	110
I Promise Never to Forget You	112
Time Slowly Passes	113
Davey's Bequest	**115**
A Kiss is All I Ask of You	118
A Kiss is All I Ask of You	119
Kiss Me Goodnight, Kiss Me Goodbye	120
Give My Love to the World	121
Forever is Now	122
Davey's Final Letter	**123**
Davey's Final Letter	126
Epilogue	**129**
Words of Hope From the Author	**133**
My Tribute to Davey	**135**
About the Author	**140**

ACKNOWLEDGEMENTS

Writing a book is a solitary experience. Delivering a book is a group experience. Words swirl through the mind and somehow end up on the page in an order that seems to make sense, at least to the writer. There is no guarantee the words will be sensible or meaningful to anyone else. The ability to be objective disappears in the wind. It is time to call in other eyes and expertise.

Given the title of this book, it is only fitting to give thanks to the Angels who helped me deliver it. Joyce Leonard shepherded the entire production and publishing process with unfailing patience and enthusiasm. Marcia Ellett, editor, and Tracey Carruthers, proofreader, treated the manuscript with understanding and respect for the heart and message of the author and the words. JD Buckwell took the reins of layout and cover design with a deep understanding of, and sensitivity to, the dual presence of beauty and love in the midst of death and destruction. Robert Garner was a continuing source of unflagging support, commitment, inspiration, vision, and creative consultation. Toni Arland saw the message, meaning, and purpose of the book long before I did.

I cannot express the measure of my gratitude to those, too numerous to mention, who took the time to listen, read, talk, share ideas, and gently push me in the direction of sharing a message that is both timely and timeless. It is humbling to be the recipient of such dedication.

No acknowledgement would be complete without recognizing Lois Haraughty. Her love, friendship, and unfailing commitment to my survival were my links to sanity and hope during and after those troubled times.

And a special thanks to Heidi Volpe who opened the door of precious memories.

PREFACE

Without warning, someone enters your life and makes such an impact it seems your world is turned upside down. The depth and breadth of the effect becomes clearer over time like extended aftershocks and reverberations from an earthquake. The significance of such powerful relationships on the heart and mind is discovered over a lifetime.

This book is about such an experience in my life, the lessons of which continue to reveal themselves to me and, I suspect and hope, always will. It's the story of the relationship between a young nurse and an even younger patient in the midst of the Vietnam War who explore lessons in life through each other's eyes. I'm the nurse and Davey is the patient.

We discussed mutual interests in creativity, art, music, dance, literature, science, and most of all the meaning of life and death. At that point, writing was my release mechanism for war's relentless assault on my senses. I wrote poetry and prose about the experiences of that intense time.

Davey was a subject and influence for writing during that period. After the war, my writing voice about that topic was silenced until I was able to look at memories of him and others and begin writing again in 2001. His was among the first memories to "require" me to write about them.

At times I discover some of the old pages of my scribbling in a long-forgotten box or desk drawer. There may well be more waiting to be unearthed from their hiding places. I hope there are.

The following pages include poems and commentary about this special patient of mine. Some are from the time I lived in that war; others are from reflections on that time written in the past few years.

I share them with you now as a tribute to the memory of this extraordinary young man who knew how to live with grace and joy all the way to the moment of his transition. His wisdom became part of my heart and soul, and he provides comfort to me always—just as he promised he would.

Penny Rock

Note: Eligibility to Vote

The Twenty-Sixth Amendment to the United States Constitution lowered the eligible age to vote from twenty-one to eighteen. It was adopted July 1, 1971. The amendment was the result of student activism against the Vietnam War and the inability to express their views in the voting booth about being conscripted to fight. President Eisenhower was the first president to publicly state his support for suffrage for those eighteen and older. The slogan "Old enough to fight, old enough to vote," dated back to WWII when President Roosevelt reduced the military draft age to eighteen.

BACKGROUND

BACKGROUND

This book is the story of an Army nurse and a soldier patient that takes place in a hospital ward during the Vietnam War. I was the nurse and Davey was the patient. But, the story didn't begin in that hospital nor did it end there.

Like any story, there is a background for the people in it. Who were these people *before* Vietnam? What quirk of fate brought two young people from disparate backgrounds together to form a relationship that seemed destined to exist? Why there? Why then? What was the lifelong significance of their meeting?

The obvious reason we met was that he was wounded and I was a nurse. He was my patient. But I had hundreds of patients that year, so what made *our* meeting so special?

We believed we met because we were kindred souls. Our lives were operating in the same sphere regardless of our physical location. We were two sides of one coin. This was our single opportunity to join the coin. *That* we would meet was not optional—it was simply a matter of *when*.

Intense circumstance requires intense presence. Half of "us" was dying, so fleeting moments needed to be captured to distill what we understood about life and to crystallize the quality of life to be lived after his departure. We understood the physical plane was going to be left solely to me, and we hoped it would be a long-term contract. My promise was to live out our dreams in a way that made our presence on earth worthwhile. His role would be to provide support, guidance, and comfort to me all the while.

Davey and I have been healing spirits for each other since those dark days of pain, uncertainty, and destruction. But, I want to introduce you to the Penny and Davey we were before our world exploded. I want to share with you our individual and mutual dreams, and how Davey kept his promise to maintain the eternal bond of our connection no matter what hurdles and barriers life provided.

It is a simple gift. The gift of our spirits to yours.

REMEMBERING DAVEY

I forgot Davey for 20 years. Oh, he would pop into my mind at times beckoning me to pay attention. I'd see his face more than hear his voice. I'd close my eyes to shut out the image that held too much pain. It didn't work. My stomach would tighten when he appeared. My hands would shake. My neck would begin to sweat. A cold tingling would creep up my spine. Still, I didn't have a clear picture of the impact he had on my life; I just knew he had one.

Certainly I knew he was housed in my memories of war. I could even recall parts of the story. Each time he invaded my mind, I shut a mental door and tried to lock it. I tried to padlock it. The image that wouldn't leave was his eyes. They looked at me with such sadness and compassion. He wanted me to recognize him—to remember him and his importance in my life. I wanted to remember. I was afraid to remember. I *did* know that when I was *able* to remember, something would shift for me—break open—and I was both intrigued and frightened.

So, I just let the subject rest. I didn't *try* to remember, but at some level, I felt it *would* happen. And the cold in my bones told me that when it did, I would not have a choice in the matter. I couldn't pick a time and place. I couldn't "will" it, nor could I escape it.

An Inconvenient Memory

Music was always a necessary part of my life. Even though singing opera was my major love, I also loved singing cabaret music—the magnificent Broadway show tunes and standards from the Great American Songbook. One of the richest creative periods of such music occurred during the years just prior to, during, and just after World War II. I loved it all.

In the late 1980s, my husband, Bob, and I went to see a production of music popular in the 1940s. The show was being presented as a radio program from that era—complete with sound effects and commercials of the time. Even better, it was being presented in a theater at the Presidio, the old Army base in San Francisco. The theater had actually been used for radio broadcasts during World War II, where Frank Sinatra and his contemporaries were regulars on the circuit.

We walked into the theater and the old music was playing in the background; photographs of military and musical luminaries lined the walls. We took our seats—second row center—and were treated to a stage set that looked exactly like an old radio set. Contraptions everywhere. Sound effects gizmos. Gigantic microphones. Lighted signs telling us "Standby," "Applause," and "On The Air." We searched the program and found a long list of favorite songs, then settled in for two hours of glorious music.

When the program was over, the musicians and singers were clearly not finished. An unlisted song was about to be played. Instruments were raised, singers approached the microphones, and the strains of "I'll be Seeing You" began. I have no memory of hearing the song. I only remember hearing the sound of someone sobbing. Then, I realized it was I who was sobbing.

I became aware of Bob leaning over me and asking what was wrong. I have no idea how long he had been doing so. I couldn't move. We sat there until others left. Bob later told me people were looking at me and asking if they could help. I wasn't aware of any of it. I was just engulfed in gut-wrenching sobs. And I didn't know why.

I gathered the strength to go to the car and, as we walked, Davey's face came into crystal clear view. I doubled over as if I'd been punched in the stomach. I *remembered* Davey. I *remembered* "I'll Be Seeing You" was his favorite song. I *remembered* him asking me to sing it to him while he was dying. I felt betrayed. Why wasn't the song listed on the program or at least announced as an encore? Why didn't they give me warning? Words came pouring out of me and Bob was left trying to assemble them into some meaningful message. That's the force with which Davey came back to me—with an insistence I couldn't ignore.

His reappearance was unexpected and unwelcome. I cried for two days. I felt depressed. My stomach ached. I couldn't eat. And sleep was just the playground of nightmares. But I had a full-time job and had to go to work. So, I sucked it up, did my job, and nobody was the wiser.

A door of my memory had been wrenched open, but only partially. I wanted to look inside but was afraid of what I might see. I needed more information about the story of Davey. And, *finally*, I remembered where to go for the answer.

Letters to Lois

My girlfriend, Lois, and I traveled to Europe for the first time when I was working at Walter Reed General Hospital. The day I returned, my orders for Vietnam were waiting for me. I called Lois and told her. We decided that if I survived my tour of duty, we would take a trip around the world immediately after my return to the States. I also extracted a promise from her that if I did not survive, she would go on the trip in remembrance of our dream.

I was the visionary and she was the planner. I'd come up with grand ideas of where to go, and what to see and do. We were always on the same wavelength; she just sometimes thought I was wild. Lois was meticulous about putting our dreams into action. But how were we going to keep the plans in motion if I was in some land across the world in the middle of a war? We came up with the brilliant idea that I would take a tape recorder with me and send her audio letters. That was how we conducted our "discussion" as we planned the trip.

In the midst of war, the tapes took on another element. They morphed from travel planning details into contemporaneous accounts of what life—and death—was like in war. For the most part, we recorded over each other on the same tape. But somehow, four tapes were kept intact. Lois kept them safe and gave them to me when I returned home.

And on those tapes was the story of Davey.

A Voice from the Past

I kept those tapes close to me for 20 years. Secured by two thick red rubber bands, they were always in the upper-right drawer of my desk at work. No matter how many desks over how many years, over how many jobs, that was their location. They were small, reel-to-reel tapes in their original mailing container. Lois' cramped handwritten address to my APO number in Vietnam was still legible. They were always by my side, but I never listened to them.

Now, in the late 1980s, it was time I did. One problem. Had the tapes degraded over the years? Would there still be sound on them? I took them to a recording studio to see if there was any hope. They said there was! Within two weeks, they had preserved the original tapes while copying the sound to cassette tapes. I took them home, stored the originals in a safe location, and placed the cassette versions in the drawer of my stereo cabinet. They stayed there for another year.

When I finally dared to listen to them, I could only do so in small doses. Hearing my disembodied young voice was strange. It sounded almost exactly as it does today. Hearing the sounds of war in the background was surreal. It took me several weeks, but I eventually listened to them in their entirety. Just as I hoped, the story of Davey became clear. And the story was told in my own voice.

I heard myself describing him, his dreams, his view of life, his last words to his family, his desire for how my life would unfold, his request that I sing his favorite songs to him as he lay dying, and his promise to watch over me after he was gone. I heard my voice sing "I'll Be Seeing You" in memory of him.

In Remembrance

In the years since I listened to those tapes for the first time, Davey has continued to reveal himself and his importance to me—his predictions and words of faith in my creative gifts, his wisdom and understanding about how to face abysmal odds with grace, hope, and passion regardless of outcome, his zest for living until there are no more moments *to* be lived. His memory certainly provided comfort and strength for me as I was treated for cancer in 1999.

I was always a writer. I wrote in my youth and while I lived in Vietnam. After my return to the States, I continued to write—but not poetry and not about war. I returned to Vietnam for the first time in 1995, and that visit resulted in three poems. But, after my bout with cancer, the floodgates opened wide, the words poured out and the subject of war was no longer verboten. The first door to open was that of poetry. And one of the first poems I wrote was dedicated to Davey—"Return to Me."

My memory of him is no longer cloudy or limited to his big blue eyes. It is crystal clear. I can see his blond hair, his narrow nose, his wounds, his fingers and toes. I see how his five pillows were arranged to accommodate the various tubes and machines trying to keep him alive. I can see him inside his body bag—my last memory of him. I can hear his voice—his impassioned strength and his fevered weakness. I can hear his last breath.

His memory is no longer painful. Quite the contrary, it gives me joy. He is my daily companion. I'm glad I finally listened to him.

I hope the spirit of this glorious young man will touch you as it does me, and give you comfort and hope and unbridled delight in the gift of life.

PENNY'S DREAM

I decided at the ripe old age of thirteen to be an opera singer. I knew I would need a "portable" career to allow me to study and support myself anywhere in the world. So, I received some scholarships and obtained a few student loans and entered nursing school immediately after graduating high school. The plan worked well until my junior year when increasing demands in school made it difficult to work additional shifts in the hospital to earn money to pay off the loans.

Enter military nurse recruiters. I decided a paycheck each month was worth a two-year obligation and signed up for the Army Nurse Corps. Nothing was mentioned about the possibility of going to war—until basic training. It then became clear it was a matter of when, not if.

I planned to study in New York, and later in Europe, to become an Opera Singer, when I completed my military obligation. Assurances were made by a prestigious school that a place would be held for me, so I went off to do my duty at the age of twenty-one.

Name That Tune

Naturally, I took sheet music to the war. I couldn't imagine not continuing to practice. The minute I landed in country, it was clear there would be no sabbaticals for music. I sang when I could, usually in my room by myself, occasionally, some little songs to settle nervous patients. Sometimes, after a shift, a group of us would get together to listen to, and sing along with, the Mamas and the Papas, the Fifth Dimension, or Petula Clark. An anesthesiologist with a good tenor arrived, and we would use any off hours to go someplace to sing our hearts out.

But Davey was my best audience. He had heard from another patient that I could sing and asked me if I knew any Broadway show tunes. A strange request from a boy with such a fragile hold on life. Thus began a ritual of little serenades for the young man who found solace in music. Yet, as much as I enjoyed honoring his requests, I noticed my voice was changing. There was a raspy quality that wasn't there before. I thought it was the effect of not being able to practice enough and properly. Or perhaps the 120-degree heat and the need for hydration played a role. No matter the cause, I couldn't do anything about it until I returned home, but the feeling troubled me.

Davey was a dancer and painter. His interest in art encompassed all forms. He studied and enjoyed the masters of music, dance, painting, sculpture, poetry, and literature. We had something to talk about beyond his deteriorating condition. He not only asked me to sing to him, he asked me to read to him—Shakespeare, Tennessee Williams, opera libretti, and Homer were among a variety of companions to join me on my exotic journey into war.

We discussed our dreams for life, completely forgetting his was near the end and mine might well be. As his strength was ebbing, he became more insistent we create a mutual pact and promise. I was to live out our dreams and he would watch over me, protect me, and keep me on track. We joked that he was taking on the role of "director" of my life.

All the War's a Stage

One evening, he had a particularly urgent message for me. He was distraught that I was in a war zone rather than on a stage. He knew I had experience as a singer, writer, and actress. He wanted to set me free from war, so I could give myself over to the creative muses. He said, "You need to sing in theaters big enough to hold your voice. You need to dance, write books, poetry, plays, and act in the great dramas. You need to tell people everywhere what we know about life and give them reason to hope. You need to be doing it now!"

I just listened. He was feverish in temperature and passion, but I realized he was on a mission and not to be interrupted. Suddenly, in an act summoning all his strength, he raised his hand, cumbersomely encased in an arm board, and pointed to the other end of the Recovery Room next to Intensive Care where he was located. "There!" he said. I looked where he pointed and saw only beds with young men in them. "There is where the stage should be. Right now. You could do it now. Why can't we do it now? I can't, but you have to promise me you will. Please promise me you will live our dreams. I'll help in my own way. I'll watch over you. I won't leave you. Just listen and watch. I won't forget you just because I'm not here. And you won't forget me either, will you?"

How could I ever forget such an extraordinary, wise, enlightened young man? I made the promise. I would remember, I would find a way to live our dreams. I would watch and listen for his "directorial" view. And definitely, I would never forget him.

I Left My Voice in Vietnam

No matter how much inspiration fuels our dreams, we don't control the outcome. Such was the case for me and my dream of singing opera.

During my one-year tour of duty in Vietnam, all my colleagues and I became ill with unknown diseases. I hadn't had much experience with tropical disease in Minneapolis. Some of the exotic infections I had attacked my vocal cords. A couple of the doctors took a look at my throat and were disturbed by what they saw. So was I. But war was not the time or place to secure a definitive answer to my mounting fears.

Soon after returning to the States, I visited a number of specialists in San Francisco. The infections had scarred my vocal cords, and I had also developed nodes. Surgery was a relatively new option, but outcomes were uncertain.

The diagnosis I feared, but expected, was confirmed. I would be unable to sing again.

Footnote

Since my original sojourn, I have returned to Vietnam twice and found what remained of my hospital and living quarters.

In 1995 I was able to visit the area that had been our operating rooms. Some of our old furniture, cabinets, and signs were still there. But, access to my wards was forbidden. They housed a sweatshop owned and operated by the South Korean government. We had no American Embassy at the time, so all attempts to gain permission were denied.

In 2005, I visited during Tet. I wanted to experience their New Year as the cultural celebration it was meant to be rather than the "offensive" it was when I lived there. With the help of Hau, my Vietnamese friend, I was able to go inside my wards. It was overwhelming on every sensory level. All the memories of that time, and of all the years since, collided in that single moment. I was on my knees lost in tears, having difficulty breathing.

A woman, who was the Police Chief for the area, entered and told me I must leave. Her hand rested on her gun, a not-so-subtle reminder of her authority. The wards were now one large room. This was the Communist Party Headquarters meeting room, and I was off limits.

I had come too far to be summarily removed from my own wards. I told my friend to tell her she would have to shoot me first. Every fiber of my being meant every single word. I don't know what Hau told her, but she looked surprised. Crazy American may have crossed her mind. She told Hau I had seven minutes. Seven minutes to drink in 35 years.

As I roamed the room, the voices, sounds, and smells of that year were present. I could see the beds and bodies. Standing where Davey died, I looked down the length of the room where he had pointed and made such a vehement plea.

The entire end of the room was...a stage.

DAVEY'S DREAM

I never saw Davey standing up. My patients weren't in an upright position. They were either face up or face down, but always recumbent. In some cases, they were elevated into a semi-sitting position.

Davey was 18, approximately six feet tall, 160 pounds, slender, muscular, with blond slightly curling hair, big blue eyes, fair skin, good cheekbones, strong jaw, and long narrow fingers. He had a soft-spoken, baritone voice. He was handsome and he was far more mature than his years.

He had a very large abdominal wound; severe damage to the small and large colon; stomach; liver; kidney; multiple shell and fragment wounds to both legs, arms, chest, and neck; a sucking chest wound from punctured lungs; and rampant infections unresponsive to targeted and broad spectrum antibiotics. Davey was dying.

Before the War

Davey came from a middle class family and had been about to go to college. He was adamantly opposed to the war but believed he had an obligation to serve. He knew he would eventually be drafted, so he decided to enlist to get his tour of duty completed and get back to school. Politically, he considered himself a liberal democrat. Davey was fascinated by Robert Kennedy and thought he had what it took to end the war and turn national attention to living without fear. He was anxious to be able to vote as soon as he could. But, Davey was not old enough to vote. He was only old enough to be killed.

His dream was to become a doctor. More specifically, a general surgeon. A maternal uncle, I believe, inspired and supported that goal. Helping people live safe and healthy lives was his idea of a life well spent. That, and dancing and any other creative enterprise. He loved music, from the Beatles to Beethoven, Gershwin to Grieg.

His family was more than blood relation. They were best friends. He enjoyed and felt blessed by his parents and younger sister and brother. He taught his siblings how to dance so they wouldn't feel awkward at social and school events. He played baseball with his brother, taught him other sports, and took him hiking. An excellent student himself, he tutored them when they needed help.

Davey would dance his mother and sister around the living room, while his father "conducted" the orchestra, located in the radio or record player, with a newly sharpened pencil. As a family, they were active in church, but Davey was ecumenical in his views. He thought Heaven was what you lived, not where you went.

So, putting his dream of a medical career on hold, he went off to war.

The Heart of War

He couldn't understand killing. After going out with his unit on maneuvers, he and some of his buddies would go to villages and hamlets to help the local people build shacks and gather food. He taught some of the women and men how to waltz—his favorite dance.

It was during one of those maneuvers that guns, grenades, mortars, and booby traps sealed his fate to meet me and to die.

I only had a short time with Davey, but the time we had was intense. There was nothing we didn't talk about. We were spiritual soul mates on an unlikely collision course in the midst of death and destruction. At least his body was in my hands at the end rather than sacrificed to the killing fields.

What I knew about Davey, I learned in the narrow space of a hospital ward. He told stories of his home life, his family, and friends. He painted mental images for me of his childhood. He described himself as a gangly little boy who liked to run through the sprinklers, and how that exasperated his mother when he had just changed clothes. He took his dog bowling and the owner never asked him to leave. He tipped over a chemistry experiment that burned the teacher's shoes. He learned to drive the new push button Dodge.

Sometimes it seemed he was watching an invisible screen with scenes of his life parading in front of him as he narrated the film for me.

Yet, with all the little details we shared about our lives, we couldn't go back in time to live it together. I never met his family. I never heard their voices. I never ate his mother's cooking. I never saw his room or touched his dog-eared books. I never listened to his favorite music. I never saw the family photos. I never saw his parents' handwriting.

These were things I couldn't do.

There were things Davey would never do again. He never left his bed. He never saw his surroundings from a sitting position. He never could be wheeled outside to see the sunshine or the stars. He never ate another meal. He never had another drink of water. He never read another book. He never had visitors. He never held a flower in his hand—except the rose I drew for him. He never waltzed with me.

Final Thoughts

As life closes down, our experiences become more focused and intense. One night, he looked across the ward and saw a curtain pulled. He knew I was behind it. When I walked by his bed, he asked if there was something he could do to help. Not sure what that would be, I asked what he had in mind. He said, "If he's not dead, maybe I could hold his hand and talk to him. If he is dead, I want to see what you do with him because you'll be doing it to me in a few days. I want to see what happens. I want to know everything." He paid attention to everything that happened on the ward and had questions about all of it. His window for learning was closing and he didn't want to miss a thing.

Another evening, the Chaplain stopped by his bed. Davey had not wanted a chaplain but was polite and spoke with him briefly, but fatigue was wearing him out. When the Chaplain walked away, Davey watched him and said, "He has a tough job." I said nobody in a hospital like this enjoys what they are called upon to do. He said, "No. I mean he doesn't understand that once we're gone, there's nothing left to fear. The only thing after this life is pure spirit. There are no religions and denominations when we're gone. I feel sorry for him because he thinks Heaven is a place and God is a person. Look at all the bodies in this ward. Each of us has a God spirit inside us. There's plenty to go around, and there's no one on this side who controls that. So, I'll send him healing thoughts. Maybe he'd call it a prayer. I just hope he'll feel less burdened."

Two days before he died, Davey said he wanted my opinion on something. The urgency was back in his eyes and in the feeble grasp of his hand. He said, "As an artist, I always liked the idea of the "healing arts." And art heals too, I think. I wanted to be a doctor. I wanted to be a surgeon. I wanted to help people the way the surgeons do here. But nothing they could do helped me. I couldn't have helped everyone either. Like the guy down there. Some doctor I'd make. All I could do was hold his hand."

I had to interrupt. "Davey, sometimes that's the best thing a doctor, or anyone else, *can* do. Sometimes it's the only thing *left* to do. That's the "art" in healing. Knowing what the best thing to do *is*. Instead of what you can do to someone's body, it's simply being with them in the last moments. Maybe the body can't be healed, but the spirit can."

"I know. I know." He sank back into his pillows a little more. Every word was an exertion. But he still had a question to ask. "I'd never have guessed it, but I've learned a lot about medicine over here; just not the way I would have wanted. This isn't how I planned it. But, Penny, you *do* know medicine, and this is what I wanted to ask you. Do you think I would have made a good doctor?" I told him I couldn't imagine a better doctor than he would have been. He settled down a bit, smiled that brilliant smile, and said, "I didn't get my dream to be a doctor, but I met you. I'll be the doctor for your spirit. I'll stay with you. And that makes it all worthwhile."

I didn't have the honor of knowing Davey in prior years, but we lived a full life together in his last weeks. The promises we made have been a foundation of strength and a beacon of hope for me. He has come back over the years to help me heal the losses, the memories, the nightmares, and to introduce me to new dreams.

He was right. Healing *is* an art. And in my book, Davey is the consummate artist.

INTRODUCTION—
IT BEGINS AT THE END

INTRODUCTION—
IT BEGINS AT THE END

One of the most beautiful moments of love and living was born in a place of hatred and dying.

Davey came to me in a body profoundly wounded and wracked with fever from systemic infection. It was clear from the moment I first examined him that he would not survive. What I didn't realize at that moment was the magnitude of impact he would have on my life.

I was an Army Nurse in Vietnam during the most significant escalation of the war and the turning point known as the Tet Offensive. It was during another offensive, in late 1967, prior to Tet, that I met Davey, who was to become my most valued teacher about life.

I worked in the Intensive Care and Recovery units, one large room affectionately known as the Hell Hole. In war, the job of a medical professional is to get patients stabilized as quickly as possible so they can be sent elsewhere for further treatment and a better chance to recover. We also needed to send patients away fast because the beds filled faster than they could be emptied. Demand far exceeded supply.

We saw the worst of the worst in our wards, and not all of them could be quickly evacuated. Davey was one of those. So, while we had just a few weeks together, it was longer than the usual patient stay. I can only assume he had a lot to teach me, so he lived a little longer.

When Davey died, he was almost nineteen. The "almost" was important to him. He was the most focused person I have ever met in terms of wisdom and understanding about what it means to be alive right until the last breath. So I think it is fitting to begin with the end of his life, which he orchestrated as much as he could, and to end with his words of wisdom about living in the present whether or not a future exists.

I SANG YOU TO DEATH

Davey was clear and determined about each aspect of his remaining life up to and including the moments before, during, and after his death. He loved all arts, and especially loved Broadway show tunes. Two of his favorites were "If I Loved You," and "I'll Be Seeing You," in that order.

When he learned I was a singer, he was overjoyed and requested that I sing both songs to him whenever I left the ward at the end of my shift.

As he drew closer to death, he claimed a firmer grip on life. Nothing escaped his scrutiny. One night, with the intensity only a fever can produce, he grabbed my hand and said he had something important to ask of me. I leaned down closer so I could hear him better, and he made these requests. He certainly understood the war would go on, regardless of what was happening to him, but if at all possible he wanted me to do the following: send a final letter to his parents, which he would dictate to me; be with him when he died; sing his songs to him while he was dying; prepare his body after death; and place him in his body bag.

He had so little time left and had taught me so much, how could I possibly refuse?

I carried out his requests to the letter. It seemed like it took forever. In fact, each request took only minutes. The entire experience with him was so intense it seemed seared in my soul.

While singing to him, it occurred to me I was singing him to death. Not just a lullaby to ease him into sleep…but to death. My voice was to be the last thing he heard.

I wrote this poem a few days after his death with the thought, hope, and belief it would keep his memory alive.

I SANG YOU TO DEATH

I sang you to death tonight
and ended with your favorite songs,
"If I Loved You"—and I do, and
"I'll Be Seeing You"—which I will someday.

You looked so peaceful Davey
when I closed your eyes.
So young and fresh and ready for life.

The sounds of war don't disturb you now.
The distant rumble and the shaking of the ground
are of no concern anymore.

I promised you I would be with you
the rest of your young life—
a promise much too easy to keep.

You said you wanted to know the truth.
But, I don't know if I was right to tell you.

I mailed your last letters home this morning
just like you asked. I included the pictures
you carried so they couldn't be lost.

Your family will know how thoughtful you were
and how much you loved them and cared about them.
Their memories of you will be touched
by your final thoughts for them.

Where did you get your gentle spirit Davey?
Will you leave some kindness behind for
those of us who might not have enough to
give to those who need it?

You knew your fatigue was different this time.
But, still the question in your eyes as you
held out your hand to me made my heart ache
so much I thought I couldn't breathe.

When I climbed into your bed and held you
in my arms, and held your hand, you seemed
so light, like a baby in my lap.

My voice wasn't steady and my tears were
splashing on your face but, you didn't seem
to mind. Maybe because you were safe
for one last time.

Did you see your mother when you looked
up into my face? What was your last thought?
I want you to travel safe and quiet
to your next life. I want you to know I'll
always remember you and how you let me be
with you at the end.

Your final smile touched my heart and you
stayed with me until the very last note.
You wanted your songs and I was privileged
to give them to you.

Thank you for letting me sing you to your final sleep.
And, remember Davey, I'll be seeing you.

LIEUTENANT ANGEL

Sometimes blessings show up in the most unlikely places. I met my soul mate in the middle of war just weeks before he would die. It seemed like blind luck. Or maybe it was written in the stars, and all we needed to do was be present for the convergence whether or not we liked the circumstances or location.

Davey and I recognized our special relationship immediately. Don't ask me why or how. I don't know—it just happened. He called me Lieutenant Angel from the moment we met. Now, it's not unusual for a nurse or any woman to be called "angel" in a war zone. It comes with the territory.

Even though he also called me by my first name, I felt humbled by the rank he bestowed on me and the reverence with which he said it. The word angel implies some precious quality of wisdom and ability to heal or restore, and I felt I had neither.

As much as I felt ill equipped to meet the standards of the name, I was honored by the title. To this day, I believe those are the sweetest words I will ever hear.

LIEUTENANT ANGEL

He knew one day he'd meet her.
He knew it from his birth.
He'd meet her face to face,
His angel here on earth.

He knew they'd be soul mates
And live life together.
He just didn't know
The length of forever.

On his way back to college
He was detoured instead.
No thought in his mind
That soon he'd be dead.

So, still in his teens
He went off to war.
His life would be changed
As never before.

He was wounded but conscious,
So he thought he'd be fine
As long as the medics
Evaced him in time.

The next thing he saw
Was a face that he knew.
His angel was living
In this Hell hole too.

He called her Lieutenant Angel
Those last weeks of his life.
He should have been her husband.
She should have been his wife.

But he was her patient
And she was his nurse.
She assessed his condition,
And it couldn't be worse.

She knew he was special
But her heart was in pain.
She knew all her efforts
Would all be in vain.

He had plans for full living.
They were plans meant for two.
So they talked of their dreams
And the things they would do.

Cut from the same cloth
Of beauty and art,
They seized life those moments
And opened their hearts.

One day he asked her
If he'd live or die.
She had to decide:
The truth or the lie.

How do you meet your soul mate
And look him in the eye?
How do you tell your soul mate
That he's going to die?

She respected this man
And told him the truth.
He would not leave alive.
He'd die in his youth.

His fervor for living
Increased in its strength.
He'd make up in value
What he was losing in length.

The length of a life
Is not its full measure.
So they filled life with living,
Because life is the treasure.

If she could stay alive
By some miraculous means,
Her purpose in life
Would be to live out their dreams.

He had faith in her courage.
She could never be daunted.
So she promised to live
All they dreamed of and wanted.

He wrote her a letter
To speak of his love.
He'd always be with her
Although from above.

He was so full of life
Right up to his death.
He lay in her arms
As he drew his last breath.

He was her patient.
She was his nurse.
He'd return to his family
Enclosed in a hearse.

He called her Lieutenant Angel
Those last weeks of his life.
He should have been her husband.
She should have been his wife.

THE DAYS OF WAR AND ROSES

THE DAYS OF WAR AND ROSES

Davey and I had so many conversations about topics most people don't discuss until old age, if then. There were no forbidden topics between us. In fact, we felt a mutual sense of urgency to talk about the meaning and purpose of life, death, war, love, art, and anything else that came to our minds.

We both had a love of the arts in all forms, and would often play with imagery in our discussions. Some of our talks inspired me to write poems I would then read to him. He loved it. Naturally, one piece of writing would stimulate another. Some poems are in his voice, some in mine, and some are a duet.

At one point, I told him about a ritual I had before singing. I always had a single deep red, fragrant rose and one white gardenia in my dressing room before a performance. Granted the dressing room might just be a converted closet and, depending on the season, another white flower might have to be an understudy for a gardenia, but they were my faithful companions before every performance. This little piece of information sent us both off on a heart-breaking, yet beautiful, journey of the senses and images to deal with subjects that were unpalatable to others. He said he wished he had roses to give me each time I sang to him, and the beauty of the rose, in stark contrast to the ugliness of war, became a symbol of how we would remain in contact after his death.

We covered the gamut from life to death to love to war to politics. We even discussed—and possibly designed—a hereafter we pledged to inhabit. There was nothing we didn't have an opinion about. The circumstances surrounding my writing were frightening, tender, disgusting, sad, and poignant. And so are my writings.

YOUR HEART IN MY GRAVE

Your face in my mind
I want to engrave.
Your heart remains with me
While I sleep in my grave.

Remember our tree house.
Remember our cave.
Remember my whispers,
And the kisses we crave.

You're my best pal.
You are my fave.
You still own my heart,
Though I'm deep in my grave.

The memories you have,
The mementos you save,
Will be all that remains
Of the life that I gave.

The tears that you weep
That come in a wave…
Just know that I love you
From the depths of my grave.

Though I want you to live,
And know that you're brave,
I wish you were with me
In the tomb of my grave.

YOUR FAVORITE ROSE

I'll be the ribbon in your hair,
The flowers in your vase,
The dancing frock you wear,
The smile upon your face.

I'll part the clouds,
To give you sun.
When you choose a love,
I'll be the one.

When you walk in your garden
To see how it grows,
You'll find that I'm
Your favorite rose.

LET MY GRAVE STAY OPEN

Please let my grave stay open.
Don't fill it with regret.
If you can look inside and see me,
I'll be harder to forget.

I want the air to fill
With the fragrance of your scent.
The memory of your voice remains,
Though my poor life is spent.

I want to see your hair
As you bend down to speak.
I'll wish for you some courage
When I see you're feeling weak.

I want to see the birds,
I want to hear their song.
I need open space to see
If you should come along.

When I am in my grave
Don't cover me with snow.
Let the ground stay open
So I can rest below.

I want to feel the warmth.
I want to see the sun.
I want to see the moon rise up
When my day is done.

When next you come to visit me,
We'll gaze into the sky.
And for a brief and tender moment,
We'll pretend I didn't die.

THE ROSE ON YOUR GRAVE

I'll be the pages in your book,
The wind in your hair.
The shadow on your wall
Will tell you I'm there.

I'll be the music you sing.
I'll be the waltz that you dance.
I'll be the portrait on your canvas.
I'll be the one you romance.

I'll be the film in your camera,
And the moments we steal.
I'll rest in your heart,
And be the love that you feel.

I'll be the glance that reminds you
Of our love born this year.
I'll be the courage you need
To stand up to your fear.

I'll be the strength you require
To hear the sad news,
Of the way your life ends
That you did not choose.

I'll be the thought in your mind
That puts you at ease.
I'll be the medicine that saves you
From war's fatal disease.

I'll be the wine in the glass
At your final Communion.
I'll be standing beside you
At our final reunion.

I'll be the mirror that shows you
That you're not alone.
I'll be the hope at your death
That you can't postpone.

I'll be the tears in your eyes
So you needn't cry.
I'll be the last breath you take
On the day that you die.

I'll be the bearer of treasures
You leave on bequest.
I'll be the angel who guides you
To your place of rest.

I'll be the ring on your finger,
And the locket in your hand.
I'll be the earth that surrounds you
Where you lie in the land.

I'll be the voice and the fragrance
And the memories you save.
You can reach up and touch me.
I'll be the rose on your grave.

MY SENSE OF YOU

I smell the fragrance of your skin
And know that you are near.

I hear the sound of your voice
And it's music to my ear.

I touch your hands
And feel safer now you're here.

I see every angle of your face
And that keeps my memory clear.

I taste the salt of tears upon your face
And try to kiss away your fear.

My senses memorize all you are
And celebrate my time with you, my dear.

LAST MOMENT

I watch you fall asleep,
No furrows on your brow.
I want to say I Love You,
I need to say it now.

I look down at your body,
I see the rise and fall of your chest.
I listen to your heartbeat,
And feel it in my breast.

I kiss your parted lips,
And hear the intake of your breath.
My head is aching with the knowledge
Of your impending death.

You have no further future.
You had so little past.
I treasure this moment of life in you
Because it is your last

ETERNAL CONNECTION

ETERNAL CONNECTION

Neither Davey nor I was satisfied with the notion that life on this earth was all there was to existence. We didn't give it a name, but we did believe that the soul mate connection between people was evidence not of humans having a spiritual experience, but of spirits having a human experience.

He pledged he would watch over me and help me through my life because he was convinced I was to remain alive to carry out the plans we made. Otherwise, why had we been thrown together so intensely? So, we explored the realm of the unknown. We decided that eternity was in the instant of now *and* throughout the great expanse we call time.

I KNOW YOU'RE WITH ME

I know you're out there.
I know you're with me.
I feel your presence
In places that surprise me.
Your spirit gives me energy.
Your soul gives me hope.
Our dreams are coming true,
As you predicted in those early years.
When we were young, we could
Afford to live in the Heaven of our fantasies,
Regardless of the Hell that surrounded us.
You tap me on the shoulder.
Your lips brush my skin.
I know they're angel kisses
Meant to soothe and give me peace.
What you've asked of me is enormous,
But never becomes a burden.
I want to do you justice,
And enrich lives around me,
As you enriched mine.
Sometimes I see shadows on the wall,
And I recognize your form.
I see reflections in a window,
And see your face next to mine.
I'd know you in a second
If you walked around the corner.
What fates brought us together?
Why there, and then, and for such a little time?
And though you had to leave and I had to grieve,
You've never really left me.

Eternal Connection

I'm young again when I think of you,
And I think of you each day and night.
No matter what I've lived through,
You've been steady by my side.
I have a special reward for you.
I'll sing to you again.
How could you be so constant?
How did I deserve such a love?
We're embarking on new ground, my dear.
I especially need you now.
I surrender to your guidance,
Because I know you're with me.

ONE BREATH AWAY

Although we have been separated
By time and years and space
Our connection just grows stronger.
I clearly see your face.

I can almost touch you.
I can almost hear your voice.
I know now our paths were set
By Divine or Cosmic choice.

I could join you in a moment
With or without pain.
A simple little nuance
Has us on a different plane.

We're separated by a heartbeat.
We're just one breath away.
We could start a new life
Together…now…today.

WE TWO ARE ONE

You come to me
In the heart of night.
My mind sees you,
And you hold me tight.

We two are one.
We two are whole.
Your spirit speaks
Right to my soul.

My heartbeat changes,
As if you're near.
Your touch is burning,
As if you're here.

WE'LL FIND US

I'll see you in the corners.
I'll meet you at the winds.
I'll catch you at the margins,
And where the sun begins.

You'll find me in blank spaces.
You'll see me floating free.
You'll hear the whisper of my voice.
That's how you'll know it's me.

I'll travel through the clouds.
I'll ride a shooting star.
I'll zig-zag down a lightning bolt
To locate where you are.

You'll see me sitting on a rainbow.
You'll find me on the moon.
You'll hear me sing from Saturn's rings,
And know me by my tune.

HAIRPINS ON THE FLOOR

She stands in the moonlight
Hair piled high on her head.
It's so close to morning
But too early for bed.

She stares into space,
Her gaze straight ahead,
With thoughts of her lover.
Her lover who's dead.

As she stares out the window
Her thoughts start to swim.
A man enters her room
And she knows that it's him.

She hears the beating of their hearts.
She hears the whir of the fan.
She's the girl inside the woman.
He's the boy inside the man.

She feels his arms around her.
She feels his love surround her.

His hands are lost inside her hair.
It spills past shoulders that are bare.

He says he'll always love her.
He says he'll never leave her.

He tells her to believe in him.
He asks her to have faith in him.

She leans against him finding strength.
She knows life's measured by more than length.

He says no matter how things seem,
Her purpose is to live their dream.

He says, "I'm always just beside you".
He says, "Just trust the voice inside you".

In the quiet of the moonlight
She listens to hear more.
She's familiar with his pattern.
It's been this way before.

Suddenly, he's gone.
No closing of a door.
Something glistens in the moonlight.
She sees her hairpins on the floor.

SHE WAITS FOR HIM

She sits sipping tea.
Lavender fills the air.
She examines her face
So light and so fair.

Her skin was once flawless.
It now shows some wear.
She wonders if he'll notice.
She wonders if he'll care.

She waits with such patience
Each night and each day.
She's hoping and praying
She'll know what to say.

When he finally appears
He'll bring back those years
When she shed all those tears
And faced all those fears.

She senses more than sees him.
Her breath catches in a sigh.
He puts his arms around her.
They both begin to cry.

His smiling eyes are like the evening sky.
His hair's still blond and curly.
She remembers how he looked at night
And when he wakened early.

He asks her if she's happy.
How can she tell him no?
They hold each other tightly
Not wanting to let go.

She holds his face within her hands.
He runs his fingers through her hair.
The tests of time and quirks of fate
Were cruelly unfair.

She spends her days and spends her nights
In the middleness of time.
The waiting is so painful.
The dreaming is sublime.

Now he stands before her.
He's come to her at last.
It's not possible to talk of future
So they cling to memories of the past.

She lives a life of waiting.
She never would complain.
The waiting seems to suit her
As her years begin to wane.

She remembers how he looked back then,
So handsome and so brave.
He hasn't aged a moment
Since she placed him in his grave.

RETURN TO ME

Return to me my love.
I never meant to leave you behind.
I never forgot your gentle touch,
The sun in your smile,
The blue sparkle in your eyes,
The golden halo of your hair.

Your heart held enough love
And compassion for all of us.
You reached out to touch me,
But I had drifted just out of reach.
How lonely you must have felt
Not knowing if our souls would join again.

How filled is your throat with songs unsung,
Your eyes with tears unshed,
Your heart with love unexpressed,
Your joy denied laughter,
Your breath without exhale,
Your skin denied touch,
Your creation unfulfilled?

Your eyes have seen too much my love,
They ask questions that have no answers.
Can you forgive me for turning my face
In silence all these years?

Do you know it's safe now
To return to me?
Do you trust I will love and nurture you
Now and forever?

Do you know my heart can hold all of you,
And you will never be alone again?
I love you more than life itself,
And I will hold your spirit
In the sanctuary of my soul.

Return to me my love,
And we'll embrace our spirits
For eternity.

WHAT MORE COULD I DO?

WHAT MORE COULD I DO?

I was Davey's nurse. Yes, we were soul mates who became fast friends and could speak the unspeakable to each other. We felt we knew each other from beyond time and wasted no time on the standard formalities of getting to know each other. We already knew each other intimately.

But, first and foremost I was his nurse with all the requisite responsibilities that go with the position. I did for him what I did for other patients. None of it was appealing, most of it was painful, and in Davey's case, all of it was futile.

No matter how much skill, ability, or knowledge any of the medical staff had, we couldn't save those whose bodies were too shattered or whose immune systems were too compromised to continue to support life. It's hard not to take that personally. I knew intellectually I had done as much as I could. But the question remained, and remains to this day, what more could I have done?

The helpless and hopeless feeling of having no control over the arbitrariness of who lives or dies is incredible. Why do two boys with the same infection or injuries have different outcomes? It's an unsolvable mystery.

The haunting part is never being able to make sense of why such promising young lives needed to be sacrificed. Was there something more I could have done? It's a question I could never answer. I still can't.

LAMENT

Life is a journey.
It was your journey.
Why did it end so soon?

With all I gave you,
I couldn't save you.
When will the nightmare end?

I see you lie here.
Why did you die here?
How can you leave me now?

I've done all I should.
I wish that I could
Breathe life into your soul.

I have regret still.
I can't forget 'till
I see your face again.

I know your heart aches.
You know my heart breaks.
When will we meet again?

I hear your heartbeat.
You took my heartbeat
And made it all you own.

What are you doing?
What can you tell me?
Should I be unafraid?

You know I miss you.
I want to kiss you.
My heart will never mend.

I have the remnants
Of sweet remembrance
Of all you could have been.

How can you hear me,
If you're not near me?
How will you know my pain?

You say you'll love me,
Though you're above me,
Throughout eternity.

You say you'll guide me.
You'll walk beside me.
How will I know you're there?

What have they done here?
I'm all alone here.
How can you help me now?

Please help me Davey.
I need some safety.
I'm caught up in a storm.

On each tomorrow,
I'm full of sorrow
For all that's happened here.

I hear the voices
Of wartime noises.
When will it ever end?

So much to grieve here.
I want to leave here.
I fear I'll disappear.

What More Could I Do?

My spirit's reeling
From shuttered feelings.
Will I be always numb?

I can't remember.
Did I surrender
To live my life in Hell?

My heartbeat races.
I see their faces
In dreams that never end.

My heart is lonely.
I've one wish only,
That I can love again.

I feel I've lost track.
I want my life back.
Who holds the key to that?

And when I wander,
I can't help wonder
If I will live again.

I've done my duty.
I know they'll judge me.
What more could I have done?

I want exemption.
I want redemption.
Oh God please help me now.

I've lost my heart here.
I've lost my art here.
Why did it have to end?

DAVEY'S WALTZ

Davey was a dancer. You name the dance and he could do it. He would dance with girlfriends, his sister, and his mother. To hear him tell it, he was a hot property on the dance floor whose dance card was always full.

He said he wished he could dance with me through the ward. I would be wearing a flowing blue dress. His favorite dance? The slow waltz.

For whatever reason, the plaintive poem Davey's Waltz came to me, at least in part, in the rhythm of a waltz. Even though the words were painful to write, I could see us swirling across the floor. Of course, we never got to dance, but I think he would be pleased that one of my poems about him is graceful in my mind's image and tone, if not in its message.

DAVEY'S WALTZ

Here are you.
Here am I.
You're the stars
In my sky.

You're the sun
That can
Melt all my fears.

I could never leave you.
You could never leave me.
We were meant to be
Just one.

I love you.
You love me.
What more
Could we be

Than two hearts
Filled with
Joy and with hope?

We just want a future.
That's just human nature.
Help us find a safe
New home.

There is evil.
There is fear.
There is death
Over here.

He Called Me Lieutenant Angel

Don't forget
Us and leave
Us to die.

We just want to live more.
They want us to give more.
What could we have done
So wrong?

We would fight
In the night
In our dreams
Full of fright

In a world
Filled with
Terror and shame.

Is there some remorse now?
There's a different course now.
Please just let us be
Reborn.

We want walks.
We want talks.
You can stop
Wartime clocks

In a world
With the strength
To forgive.

Can you just release now?
It is time for peace now
In a world ready to
Be free.

What More Could I Do?

You loved me.
I loved you.
What more
Could we do

In a world
Filled with
Pain and despair?

I just want to hold you.
Have I ever told you
You have made my life
Worthwhile?

You had life.
You had breath.
Now I hold
You in death

In my arms
Filled with
Sorrow and tears.

I tried to save you.
I'm afraid I failed you.
Do you think you can
Forgive?

You are gone
With my soul.
Will I ever
Be whole

In a world
That is lonely
And cold?

I will not forget you.
I could never let you
Think you lived your life
In vain.

It has been
A long while
Since I've seen
Your sweet smile

In a world
Filled with
Sadness and loss.

I just want to touch you.
I just want to hold you.
I just want to
Kiss you hello.

You live on
In my heart.
We will not
Be apart

In a world
That we fill
With our love.

I still hold you safely
Here within my memory.
You were God's blessing
To me.

LIFE INTERRUPTED

LIFE INTERRUPTED

When we are in the prime of youth, all attention is on the future; what we will study, what we will do, what we will be. Thoughts are filled with images, dreams, and fantasies of the life ahead of us. There is one underlying assumption—that we actually do have a future.

In the days of my youth, there was an ominous piece of background music playing in our lives known as the Draft. Boys were assigned a number in this giant lottery and sooner or later the long arm of the government would reach out and pluck them from their homes and send them to what seemed like another planet. All their plans, hopes, dreams, and indeed their lives were interrupted. For some, it would be permanent. When they stepped on the plane that would take them to war, they assumed they would eventually come back to the "world." They just didn't know in what condition they would return. Or when.

THE WAR GOT IN THE WAY

As young adults, we have big plans about what life has to offer us. Then suddenly, in the midst of those plans, we are sent off to war. In an instant, life as we know it or imagined it to be has changed forever. Unlikely friends and lovers show up in our lives only to be blown to bits in front of us. All our plans and hopes and things we thought we could count on are ripped from our hands and hearts in a moment. Nothing is the way we thought it would be. Nothing is the way it should be.

THE WAR GOT IN THE WAY

I met a young man in a foxhole.
We were buddies the very first day.
We made plans for later in life.
But the war got in the way.

My friends blew up beside me.
I'd crawl through the mud and pray.
Life was ending all around us.
I hoped some of us could stay.

I went out on daily maneuvers
Seeking an enemy to slay.
We were all just boys not wanting to die.
But the war got in the way.

I counted hours, days and months;
Tossed calendar pages away.
I didn't know if Mom's cross was lucky,
But I wore it anyway.

I described the war in my letters.
I told what we endured every day.
But they chastised me for cowardice,
And political rhetoric held sway.

I desperately wanted to go home
To be embraced in the American way.
Then I heard we might not be welcome,
Hated for our role in their play.

I only wanted to tell the truth.
There was so much I wanted to say.
And then their letters stopped coming,
Though I waited for them each day.

I actually thought I might make it,
But was suddenly caught in the fray.
Bullets, rockets, and mortars
Were coming directly my way.

I flew in the air and rolled in the dirt,
I was stuck in the mud and the clay.
I heard groans, cries, and engines.
Then the choppers whisked me away.

They said I'd be safe in hospital,
That danger would be kept at bay.
Then bright lights shone above me,
As I lay on a big metal tray.

I just wanted to be of service.
How had my world gone astray?
I'd hoped to live a long life.
But the war got in the way.

When I woke I saw doctors and nurses
With new orders for me to obey.
But the news wasn't good for my future.
I'd be leaving without much delay.

Had I failed family expectations?
Was I a coward on my final day?
How sad if the only remembrance of me
Was a colorful funeral spray.

I met a young nurse and I loved her.
I thought of her night and day.
I dreamed of our life together.
But the war got in the way.

FUNERAL PLANS

Young people still in or barely out of their teens don't normally discuss their funeral plans. They shouldn't have to. But life in war is lived in compressed time. Each moment can be agonizingly long. Each lifetime can be over in a moment. Everyone living in a war zone is acutely aware of the random nature of injury and of who would live or die—or wish they had.

Davey had an intense curiosity about everything, so we discussed the details of what happens during and after death. And then we planned our own funerals. We wanted them to be celebrations of what little life we had lived at that point. I wanted my ashes to be taken to numerous locations around the globe. He wanted some of his ashes buried near his family, some to be taken to places he would never have the opportunity to visit, and some to be sent to me.

And finally, we developed a list of music we wanted played at our memorial services. Music was an important part of our lives and it had to play a dominant role in the final send-off.

I'll never know if he got all his wishes. I never received any ashes. I do have the memory of the beauty and heartbreak of those conversations—and I still have my plans.

FUNERAL PLANS

We're much too young for marriage,
So wedding plans aren't meant to be.
But, we're just the right age to be killed.
So it's funeral plans for you and me.

They'll have to register our names
In a room just down the hall.
I know there'll be a body bag.
Will one size fit us all?

I've nothing left for a bequest,
So I'd like to make a last request.
Since our time in life is gone forever,
May we share one coffin wrapped together?

They'll leave us all alone in there.
I wonder for how long.
Then they'll send us to our families.
I hope they can be strong.

Will there be a long procession?
Will people come to see us off?
What will be our next life?
Or have we lived enough?

I wonder if they'll speak of us.
I wonder how we'll be described.
I wonder if they'd say different things
If we had survived.

They'll finally have to lower us
Into the gaping hole in the ground.
The only evidence of our existence
Will be that pitiful little mound.

They'll carve our names and dates on stone
To prove that we were here.
If they visit us and read those words
Will they feel that we are near?

How long before we decompose?
How long until our souls leave us?
How long before we get to Heaven?
How long will people grieve us?

How long will they remember us?
How soon do memories fade?
Will they have the strength to honor
All the promises they made?

Will they remember how we look
Without aid of pictures in a book?
Will they remember how we sound
After placing us in the ground?

Will they read and read our letters?
Will they understand what we tried to say?
Will they know we tried to live our very best
When they can't see us every day?

Our life's travels now are over.
Our new home is mother earth.
All we can ever hope for
Is that our lives were of worth.

There's one thing left to say to you.
It is my last endeavor.
I loved you then, I love you now,
I'll love you for forever.

PENNY'S AND DAVEY'S FUNERAL PLANS

In those days, funerals were the expectation when someone died. There was a format of ceremony that was considered appropriate. Davey and I didn't want a funeral based on the public norm. We wanted a celebration of life rather than a mourning of death. We wanted art—in the form of paintings and sculpture; poetry; and, of course, music. And naturally, Davey wanted to add dance to the program.

Art

How do you have an art exhibition if you have no money? We thought about slides, but that too required money, and seemed like a big production. The last thing family and friends need at a funeral is more work to do. We thought about having the service in a museum, but what if they didn't have the kinds of paintings we wanted?

We finally settled on travel posters and post cards. It was genius, because the posters could also be of places I had traveled and places he wanted to see but couldn't. We would have posters and cards of the works of van Gogh, Rembrandt, Monet, Renoir, Corot, and a host of others. I wanted a picture of Rodin's Cathedral—his sculpture of two intertwined hands. I'd include our list on my next tape to Lois, and through her sources, she'd get it handled.

Poetry

There were no libraries nearby, so we looked through the books I brought with me and selected an even half-dozen.

Christina Rossetti: "Remember"
William Shakespeare: "Our Revels Now Are Ended"
    (Tempest, act 1V, Scene 1)
Alfred Lord Tennyson: "Crossing the Bar"
Emily Dickinson: "Because I Could Not Stop for Death"
Helene Johnson: "Invocation"
Robert Louis Stevenson: "Away with Funeral Music"

Music

This might have been the most difficult category because there was too much from which to choose. As we fleshed out further details in our plans, we couldn't help but laugh, because we realized the event seemed more like a concert and exhibition than a memorial service. We compiled a list that would make any orchestra proud. We each wanted some of the same music and a few highlights of our own.

Here is our initial program:

Barber: "Adagio for Strings"
Mahler: "5th Symphony; Adagietto movement"
Massenet: "Meditation from Thais"
Gounod: "Ave Maria" (for me)
Schubert: "Ave Maria" (for him)
Robert Wright & George Forrest – based on Borodin:
    "And This is My Beloved" (for me)
Irving Kahal & Sammy Fain: "I'll Be Seeing You" (for him)
Handel: "Largo from Xerxes" (for me)
Debussy: "Claire de Lune" (for him)

Pachelbel: "Canon in D" (without the Gigue)
Puccini: "Vissi D'Arte from Tosca" (for me)
Puccini: "Un bel Di" from Madama Butterfly
Vitale: "Chaconne"
Liszt: "Consolation #3"
Bizet: "Duet from The Pearl Fishers"

Dance

Davey was definite about this request. He wanted his brother and sister to waltz at his funeral. He would let them choose the waltz, but he wanted her to wear a blue dress—much like the one he dreamed of me wearing if we had been able to waltz together.

We both realized these plans could not be implemented for Davey, but just expressing his wishes seemed to be enough. He was delighted with the dream that the final experience of him could be a celebration of art.

My plans are still intact with some revisions over the years. But, these original plans will remain the foundation for my final exit because they were born in those moments of the knowledge of his imminent death, uncertainty about my own, and love for the gift of life.

A LESSON AND A PROMISE

A LESSON AND A PROMISE

Whatever the reason Davey and I were brought together, I will always think of him as one of my wisest, most insightful teachers. Even as he lay dying, he was fully engaged in life and completely generous in sharing his understanding. Maybe his understanding was so much clearer because he was so close to departure from this life. For me, he was a safe harbor in a turbulent storm. He was the only one with whom I could explore the depths of my thoughts, feelings, and questions.

I learned lessons that have served me throughout my life, and just as he promised he would never leave me, I promised to hold him and our time together in the sacred confines of my memory.

I LEARNED ABOUT LIVING

I learned about living
From a boy who was dying.
We shared in our giving
With both of us crying.

We tried to believe
He'd get a reprieve.
But his fate was leaving,
And my fate was grieving.

We made plans for great beauty
Which now are my duty.
I must be alive
For our dreams to survive.

He was a boy meant to dance,
To have love and romance.
But we both lost our chance
When death took its stance.

He said "Heaven's bells ring
When I hear you sing".
So his love of a song
Would send him along.

We knew from the start
We shared but one heart.
We became more than whole
When we merged our two souls.

It would soon be too late
For us to create.
So we dreamed of a way
For his spirit to stay.

We knew that our art
Grew deep in the heart.
We must quickly get started
Before he departed.

He said while I was young
There were songs to be sung.
And my later life's message
Would make use of war's presage.

He said I must use
His spirit as muse,
So projects could choose me
And all art forms could use me.

If I listen to him only
He'll guide me with care.
He'll give me new voice
For the message I'll share.

He said he'd be with me
In rooms and dark hallways.
I would see him in nature.
He'd be with me always.

The words that he spoke
Before his last breath,
Were words I could live by
Long after his death.

To know we can love
Is spiritually freeing.
The sharing of love
Is our purpose for being.

I PROMISE NEVER TO FORGET YOU

I promise never to forget you.
You were etched in my heart and mind.
I trusted in your vow to never leave me
Without regard for flesh and earth.

And then I was distracted,
Your loss a wound too deep to heal.
I turned my eyes to the future
Not realizing you were with me still.

I wondered why I was lonely
As I lived a crowded life.
Everywhere I looked I encountered you,
On the street, in my dreams, in my mirror.

I felt your need for recognition
But I couldn't say your name.
I sometimes saw an apparition,
Not knowing if it was you or me.

Your eyes were filled with longing.
Do you lament the silence through the years?
I sense your readiness to return,
Or am I only now ready to receive?

You have been sealed
In the closet of my memory.
Only recently released to
Experience fresh discovery.

You occupy my heart and soul,
Your voice waiting to be heard.
I promise never to forget you.
I'll listen to your every word.

TIME SLOWLY PASSES

Time slowly passes
Like water poured from glasses.
And all the while,
The memory of your smile
Comes back to me
Gentle as a touch upon my knee.

Your voice was music to my ear.
Your picture brings a little tear.
Though one of us is older,
Your presence just gets bolder.
The thought of you brings back my youth,
And urges me to speak our truth.

I can speak, but can they hear?
Can they listen through their fear?
If they close their ears and shut their eyes,
They'll be deaf and blind to mortal cries.
I expected enemies to defy me,
I never guessed my country would deny me.

I look into my mirror.
I've tried to live with grace.
The signature of time
Is written on my face.
No matter how I try,
I can't forget that place.

All these years I've waited
For someone to say they cared.
And now I finally realize.
They're silent because they're scared.

DAVEY'S BEQUEST

DAVEY'S BEQUEST

When you are a teenager dying in a hospital bed in the midst of war, possessions are at a minimum. Maybe you have a few pictures, but most of your belongings are being kept in a quasi-shrine in your room at your parents' house. In your hospital bed, the only thing you are wearing is the only jewelry you own—your dog tags.

If you know you are dying and have the time to make bequests, what do you leave—and to whom? Difficult questions, especially for someone so young. But Davey had an enlightened view about what he could leave, and he told me exactly what his bequest would be. None of it was tangible.

He left behind a spirit of hope, and honor, and love. He left words of wisdom and inspiration. He loved life and knew that each moment counted, and in his final frailty, this understanding was on his mind. It is what he wanted to share with the world at the end of his visit on this earth. I'm honored to share it with you now.

A KISS IS ALL I ASK OF YOU

No matter how many people are in beds all around you, a hospital ward is a lonely place. Sometimes the smallest act of kindness or tenderness can mean the world to a soldier who thinks he may be treading water between life and death. In those moments, the frailty of the human body knocks the stuffing out of a soldier's warrior bravado.

They shyly ask…if it's not too much trouble…if it won't get you in trouble…if no one is looking…please don't tell my buddy…would you please…maybe…give me just a little kiss…if it's not too much trouble, Lieutenant?

It's such a little thing to ask for in such a grisly place. It's a gesture that seems so simple and yet has great meaning for the moments, months, and years ahead because it recognizes the basic human need to feel loved.

A KISS IS ALL I ASK OF YOU

A kiss is all I ask of you
To remember who you are.
To hold you in my thoughts
When you have gone afar.

A kiss is all I ask of you
To give my eyes and lips a smile.
To keep the image of you fresh
And let you stay with me awhile.

A kiss is all I ask of you
To keep us close when we're apart.
The memory of your lips on mine
Warms the margins of my heart.

A kiss is all I need from you
To have hope we will survive.
Your kiss is all the evidence I need
To know that once we were alive.

KISS ME GOODNIGHT, KISS ME GOODBYE

Kiss me goodnight,
I'm lonely in this bed.
I long for human touch,
A kindness not propelled by duty.

Hold my hand and smooth my skin.
Look in my eyes and see me there.
Whisper in my ear, a tender word will do.
Hold me in your arms,
Don't let me slip away unattended.

But, if I must go,
Let me leave touched by the lips of an angel.
Kiss me goodnight.
Kiss me goodbye.

GIVE MY LOVE TO THE WORLD

Give my heart to my mother,
Since she gave it life.

Give my courage to my father,
So he can carry on.

Give my knowledge to my sister,
To help her learn of life.

Give my faith to my brother,
To help him feel secure.

Give my hope to my friends,
To help them build a future.

Give my love to the world,
In thanks for my time here.

FOREVER IS NOW

Forever is not the passage of years.
Forever is the moment of now.

Forever occurs in the instant.
And the instant of forever is now.

The mistake is waiting to live life.
Life is living us now.

You cannot wait for forever.
Forever is happening now.

DAVEY'S FINAL LETTER

DAVEY'S FINAL LETTER

In his final days, Davey was too weak to speak very much, but he still had a mission to accomplish. He asked one of our wonderful corpsmen to write a letter to me, which he dictated. It's a short, beautiful letter that he whispered a few words at a time. At the end, he mustered the strength to sign the letter himself—a feat of which he was incredibly proud.

I've included a copy of this handwritten letter as a more personal introduction to this remarkable young man. The corpsman, in tears as he wrote the letter, was so honored to have been entrusted with the task. I hope you can see Davey's strength and spirit in his signature. He'd be delighted to know that you could.

My Dearest Lt. Angel
    Penny
You wrote all the other letters for me so now Jim is writing this for you. I wish I had written it earlier when I had more strength. It may be the most important letter because you've been with me in my most intense moments of living including my dying.
How can I thank you for all you've done for me? Your love and your music are the best things anyone could offer another person. You really are my angel and I've never doubted it for a minute. I wish I could take you with me (or better yet ~~take you with me~~ stay with you) but I promise to keep my word and watch over you and come back to you often during your incredibly long life.
I love you so much. My heart is so full of you. I really do know you love me too. Keep me in your heart always and I know we'll both be safe forever.
I love you my bright shiny Penny angel
                                    Danny

I signed this myself

My Dearest Lt. Angel

Penny

You wrote all the other letters for me so now Jim is writing this for you. I wish I had written it earlier when I had more strength. It may be the most important letter because you've been with me in my most intense moments of living including my dying.

How can I thank you for all you've done for me? Your love and your music are the best things anyone could offer another person. You really are my Angel and I've never doubted it for a minute. I wish I could take you with me (or better yet ~~take you with me~~ stay with you) but I promise to keep my word and watch over you and come back to you often during your incredibly long life.

I love you so much. My heart is so full of you. I really do know you love me too. Keep me in your heart always and I know we'll both be safe forever.

I love you my bright shiny Penny Angel.

Davey

I signed this myself

EPILOGUE

EPILOGUE

Davey died relatively early in my tour of duty in Vietnam. From the moment I landed "in country" I knew I was in Hell. I was certain that if people back in the "world" just knew the truth of what was taking place, the war would come to an end. It didn't take long to realize how wrong I was.

Before I arrived in Vietnam, I knew there were protests about the war, but after I was in country we began getting word that the protests were escalating as the war did, and the dialogue between the citizenry and the government was at an all-time low.

But some part of me remained committed to being one of those who would tell the simple truth of what happens to people in war—the destruction of youth, on both sides, when the mission is to kill or be killed; the grotesque injuries; the smell of burning flesh; the piles of dead and wounded—sights and sounds nobody should see or hear.

You already know Davey and I made promises to each other, and one of the promises I made was to speak about the war. I was committed to telling my story to family, friends, organizations, newspapers, schools—anyone who would listen.

As the months wore on, so did my resolve. When I finally returned, it wasn't to the world I left. Or more to the point, I wasn't the same person I was before. With the exception of one friend, I could not make my voice heard. It wasn't welcome and neither was I. I tried several times during that first year, but to no avail. I, along with so many others, was incarcerated behind a wall of deaf ears, blind eyes, cold hearts, and closed minds.

I had made earnest promises to Davey to speak of what we saw and to remember all that we had planned. It was too painful to live with the knowledge I was a non-person, or worse, a traitor. So I placed Davey in a deep recess of the closet of my mind and locked the door. Thus began 25 years of nightmares and silence.

WORDS OF HOPE FROM THE AUTHOR

The silence did eventually end, replaced with a renewed sense of duty to pay tribute to the spirit of life regardless of co-existing trauma. I've had a wonderful, productive life, and I have always made use of the lessons I learned about life in that land of death. I never lost hope, but I was confused about whether it was too late to speak, or if anyone would actually want to hear.

I finally decided I had a voice and should use it, and it didn't really matter if anyone wanted to listen. There are still many who do not wish to hear what people like me have to say. So be it. I'm grateful the doors of my memory finally opened—and once opened, they will not be shut again.

Given the surreal environment of the wartime setting of the poems and commentary in this book, I hope this short journey through some of my experiences with Davey brings you hope, joy, and comfort. I realize that may sound strange, but I believe that regardless of the magnitude of tragedy, it's worth excavating the rubble to locate the blessings inside—no matter how long it takes to do it.

I think we need to listen to the wisdom of those voices in the wind asking us to find ways to celebrate life without sanctioning its untimely expenditure. Our job is to offer hope, understanding, and compassion so we don't perpetuate the myth that underlies all wars—that some people are more worthy of life than others. Our privilege and responsibility, as Davey so beautifully put it, is to give our love to the world—truly a bequest that can never be exhausted.

MY TRIBUTE TO DAVEY

MY TRIBUTE TO YOU, DAVEY

Hi, Davey. What can I say but thank you? Thank you for all you taught me about life and love. Thank you for letting me be with you at the end. Thank you for seeing, believing, honoring, and enriching my purpose in life. Thank you for your wisdom and guidance through tough times. Thank you for watching over me through the years.

You do know, don't you, that this book is not only *about* you, it's a *tribute* to you. It's a tribute to what your spirit offered me. My hope and purpose in writing it was to let your spirit and wisdom touch a wider audience. To let them get to know you—even a little—and be moved to discover the Davey inside them. There are still people in the world who are suffering. And in the name of suffering, they do destructive things. You know that even better than I. And, we both know it isn't possible to have *too much* love and compassion in the world. I truly believe that anyone who reads or touches this book will be the better for it. Just think of it, Davey. You can reach out through time and touch their hearts just as you did mine.

Everything I've done and how I've lived has been part of my journey to fulfill my promise to you. Of course, this book is only a small portion of that promise. But, it's special to me *because* it's a tribute to you. It has brought me such joy. Sometimes I think it might be the *best* thing I've done. It's the most gratifying. It's the most personal.

And it's not over. We have a lot more to do, Davey. Promises never expire. So, let me have one night of restful sleep. Please. Then, Lt. Angel will be reporting for duty once again. With you by my side, there's always a new adventure into the unknown, and I'm glad of it. There is one thing I do know, though. I'll be seeing you, Davey!

PRODUCTS AND SERVICES

Products
Books:
We Declare: The Truth About War and Our Responsibility for Peace
He Called Me Lieutenant Angel: A Love Song From War
Power of a Clear Mind: The Direct Link Between Your Leadership State of Mind, The Decisions You Make, The Actions You Take, The Results You Get

Audio CDs:
Power of a Clear Mind: Keep Your Bearings in *Any* Circumstance
The 8 Essential Ingredients of Healing: From *Anything, Anywhere, Anytime*

Services
Executive Consulting & Coaching: Individual and Executive Teams
Transfer of Competency: Workshops for Consultants and Coaches
Speaker: Key-Note and Conference Speaker

Learn More
To order or to learn more about Penny's Products and Services, visit: www.powerofaclearmind.com
Penny may be contacted directly at: penny@powerofaclearmind.com

ABOUT THE AUTHOR

Penny Rock is an Executive Consultant and Coach, Vietnam War Veteran, Breast Cancer Survivor, Inspirational Speaker, and Author.

Penny is the author of the books, *He Called Me Lieutenant Angel: A Love Song from War*, *We Declare: The Truth About War and Our Responsibility for Peace*, and *Power of a Clear Mind: The Direct Link Between Your Leadership State of Mind, the Decisions You Make, The Actions You Take, The Results You Get*. She has recorded the audio CDs, *Power of a Clear Mind*, and *The 8 Essential Ingredients of Healing*.

Penny was featured in the Academy Award nominated documentary film, *A Healing*, and was the inspiration for Normi Noel's play, *No Background Music*, originally produced at Shakespeare & Company in August 2006. *No Background Music* was adapted for BBC World Wide Radio, premiered in September 2005, and won the Sony Gold Drama award in 2006. Penny is portrayed by Sigourney Weaver.

www.ingramcontent.com/pod-product-compliance
Lightning Source LLC
Chambersburg PA
CBHW071702040426
42446CB00011B/1871